Voiceplay

Songs by Alison Street and Linda Bance

Illustrated by Laure Fournier

MUSIC DEPARTMENT

OXFORD
UNIVERSITY PRESS

Copy kitten

Copy kitten, copy kitten,
miaow, miaow, hiss!
Copy kitten, copy kitten,
sounds like this!

Sit by me

If you want to sing a song,
sing a song, sing a song.
If you want to sing a song,
sit by me.

If you want to play a drum,
play a drum, play a drum.
If you want to play a drum,
sit by me.

What shall I find?

What shall I find in my birthday present?
What shall I find in my birthday present?
What shall I find in my birthday present?
Early in the morning.

Let's all play with my birthday present,
let's all play with my birthday present,
let's all play with my birthday present,
early in the morning.

Barney Bear

Barney Bear is walking,
walking, walking.
Barney Bear is walking,
walking to the park.

Barney Bear has found a friend,
Barney Bear has found a friend,
Barney Bear has found a friend,
going to the park.

Sally go round the sun

Sally go round the sun,
Sally go round the moon,
Sally go round the chimney pot
on a Thursday afternoon. *Boom*!

On a log

On a log, Mister Frog,
sang his song the whole day long,
glumf, glumf, glumf, glumf!

In a pen, Missus Hen,
clucked around and scratched the ground,
squawk, squawk, squawk, squawk!

In a hole, Mister Mole,
curled up tight and slept 'til night,
snore, snore, snore, snore!

Five icicles

Five icicles, five icicles,
five icicles hanging around.
One melted—*mm*!

Under the cover

I am hiding under the cover,
under the cover, under the cover.
I am hiding under the cover,
guess how I will be?

I'll be very, very happy,
very, very happy,
that's how I will be!

Lula's lullaby

Rock-a-by, lullaby,
my baby sleep-a-by.
Stars in the sky-a-by,
twinkle goodnight.

Rock-a-by, lullaby,
why do you cry-a-by?
I love you so, and I
kiss you goodnight.

Gingerbread Man

Run, run, run,
as fast as you can,
you can't catch me
I'm the Gingerbread Man.
Little old woman and little old man,
you can't catch me
I'm the Gingerbread Man!

The wolf's tale

I'm a big, bad wolf,
my name is Keith,
I'll tell you my adventures.
I huffed and I puffed 'til I blew out my teeth
and I had to get new dentures.
So now I cannot huff,
and now I cannot puff,
I am no longer snappy.
I moved in with the little pigs,
and we're really, really, really, really happy!

OXFORD
UNIVERSITY PRESS

Great Clarendon Street, Oxford OX2 6DP, England
198 Madison Avenue, New York, NY10016, USA

Oxford is a registered trade mark of Oxford University Press
in the UK and in certain other countries

ISBN 0–19–321061–4   978–0–19–321061–5

Acknowledgements
The publisher is grateful for permission to reproduce the following poem:

Kaye Umansky: 'The Wolf's Tale' from *Nonsense Animal Rhymes* by Kaye Umansky (OUP, 2001),
by permission of Oxford University Press.

Contents

About the author

Vanessa Harrison is a member of the ColorCards editorial team. An experienced speech & language therapist, she is interested in the development of high quality, motivating resources for teaching and therapy programmes.

Introduction

olorCards is a series of language cards developed with professionals in mind. The addition of ColorLibrary, Pocket ColorCards, Illustrated ColorCards and ColorCards Games ensures that it is a creative, modern and versatile teaching and therapy tool. This handbook sets out new ideas for using ColorCards. These are in addition to the activities in the booklets included in every pack.

None of these activities are prescriptive. They are outlines to achieve particular therapeutic and teaching aims. You should adapt them to your students' needs, and then perhaps develop them further. You will find this handbook a helpful resource in every setting. The activities work well for groups and for individual students.

Some ColorCards sets have been designed with particular objectives in mind and others have a more general application. This book includes activities for ColorCards sets published up to 2006, but the ideas that it contains can also be used with sets to be published in the future.

The book is addressed to a variety of professionals working with a range of students; from the very young learning basic communication and language skills, to the older person with learning difficulties or learning English as a second or foreign language. Some users will be looking for therapeutic techniques, and others will need teaching ideas. From the 101 activities within the book you will find ideas and techniques to motivate your students, and to achieve your aims.

Using this handbook

The activities are grouped in sections under the following headings:

1	Attention	**6**	Turn-taking
2	Listening	**7**	Classification
3	Understanding	**8**	Expression
4	Auditory Memory	**9**	Using Language
5	Sequencing	**10**	Life Skills

These headings are a general classification to give some structure to the content. However, as each activity involves the practice of more than one skill, you can use many of them for other teaching aims if you make small changes. Suggestions for particular uses are included in the index at the back of the book.

Each section starts with simple activities. Harder ones follow on. They are set out to use with groups, sitting at a table. For work with individual students, simply take part in the activity yourself, as well as lead it.

You will be able to adapt almost all of the activities to make them easier or harder. You can also change the vocabulary and the emphasis to correspond to your teaching aims.

The handbook is user-friendly, with every activity clearly laid out in the following scheme:

- Number and name of activity
- Aim
- Cards to use
- Other equipment (when needed)
- Instructions for the activity (with examples if helpful)
- Word lists (where relevant)
- Suitable sets to use
- Tip (for some activities)
- Use also for (when the activity develops more than one skill)

For simplicity, throughout the book, 'you' refers to the user, and 'he' to a student.